Original title:
Candlelit Frost

Copyright © 2024 Swan Charm
All rights reserved.

Author: Paula Raudsepp
ISBN HARDBACK: 978-9916-79-666-5
ISBN PAPERBACK: 978-9916-79-667-2
ISBN EBOOK: 978-9916-79-668-9

A Soft Glow Amidst the Chill

In twilight's grasp, a whisper glows,
A lantern's warmth, as evening flows.
The stars emerge with gentle grace,
While shadows dance in quiet space.

The breath of winter, crisp and clear,
Embraces light, draws us near.
With every flicker, hearts ignite,
A soft glow, amidst the night.

Frosted Whispers of the Flickering Flame

A flame that dances, bright and bold,
Whispers secrets, tales untold.
Frosted edges, candle's breath,
A warmth that fights against the death.

In silent whispers, shadows play,
The night's embrace, they gently sway.
Flickering light, a beacon's call,
In frosted air, we find our all.

Dancing Lights on a Silent Night

Beneath the moon, the lights cascade,
In twinkling patterns, softly laid.
Silent night, a magic spell,
Where dancing lights begin to swell.

The world transforms, in hues of blue,
As stars above flicker into view.
Each glimmer sings a lullaby,
A serenade beneath the sky.

The Light that Warms the Frozen Air

From hearth to heart, a fire glows,
In every spark, a warmth flows.
The frozen breath of winter's chill,
Is softened now by fire's thrill.

In quiet corners, shadows play,
As flickers guide us on our way.
A gentle light, a trusted friend,
In frozen air, our souls will mend.

Illuminated Hues in Frosty Stillness

In the hush of winter's pail,
Colors dance, soft and pale.
Whispers of light in the air,
Gentle hues, crystal fair.

Trees wrapped in blankets of white,
Glisten quietly in twilight.
Shadows stretch, dreams take flight,
Under the stars, pure delight.

Footsteps crunch on a frosty lane,
Echoes of laughter, sweet refrain.
Nature's art, a tranquil show,
In the stillness, hearts aglow.

Mountains wear their snowy crown,
While the world slips gently down.
Each breath a cloud, soft and light,
In this magical, serene night.

As dawn breaks, colors ignite,
Painting the sky, day takes flight.
Illuminated in the still,
Frosty beauty, hearts to fill.

Dreams Entwined with the Midnight Sun

Midnight whispers secrets sweet,
Where daylight and darkness meet.
Shadows weave through the bright,
As dreams dance in the night.

Stars above, like jewels twinkling,
In quiet hearts, hope is sinking.
With each pulse, the world spins wide,
Fleeting moments, time can't hide.

Silvery beams touch the ground,
In this silence, magic is found.
Lost in thoughts, the mind will roam,
Finding in twilight, a fleeting home.

As dawn inches near, they blend,
Past and future, they transcend.
Golden rays break the dark's run,
Awakening dreams with the sun.

Love's embrace in the chill air,
Every heartbeat whispers care.
Together in this woven dream,
Life flows by in a soft gleam.

Radiant Echoes of an Icy Serenade

In the hush, a song takes flight,
Icy notes in the pale moonlight.
Breath of winter, crisp and clear,
Echoes floating, drawing near.

Snowflakes twirl in a ballet grand,
Whispering secrets to the land.
Softly calling, through the trees,
Nature sings on the icy breeze.

Echoes ripple through the night,
Chilling hearts in pure delight.
Each sound a story, softly spun,
Radiant magic has begun.

Frosted branches sway in time,
To winter's tune, a gentle rhyme.
Underneath the stars that gleam,
We find solace in this dream.

As the night begins to fade,
In the dawn, the silence made.
Echoes fade with the morning light,
Leaving warmth in the retreating night.

Warm Sighs in the Winter's Grip

Beneath the frost, beneath the snow,
Hearts find warmth in the cold's glow.
Whispers shared by the fireside,
In winter's grip, love can't hide.

Fingers tracing patterns in glass,
Moments cherished as they pass.
Each breath a sigh, a promise made,
In icy stillness, fears allayed.

Soft blankets wrap like tight hugs,
Cocoa kisses and happy shrugs.
Together we fight the chilling breeze,
Finding comfort in gentle ease.

As embers crackle, shadows dance,
In the warmth, we find our chance.
To dream, to laugh, to simply be,
In this season, it's you and me.

With every winter's lingering night,
Together we spark a tender light.
Warm sighs echo, joy's sweet grip,
In love's embrace, we will not slip.

A Flicker of Hope in Icy Existence

In shadows deep, where silence lies,
A whisper stirs beneath the skies.
The breath of dawn meets frosty air,
As dreams awaken from despair.

A flicker glows in winter's breath,
Defying cold, it dances yet.
With each small spark, the night does fade,
A promise held, the light conveyed.

Through barren woods and frozen streams,
The heart remembers tender dreams.
With every step, the chill lets go,
A fragile warmth begins to grow.

As time unfolds, the world transforms,
Revealing life in hidden forms.
The icy grip gives way to light,
A hopeful dawn breaks through the night.

In every heart, a tale does bloom,
Of seeking joy beyond the gloom.
In winter's grasp, we find our way,
A flicker's glow brightening the day.

Alight in the Quiet of Winter's Hold

In winter's hush, the world does sleep,
Where secrets in the stillness creep.
Soft crystals fall from silent skies,
As dreams take flight with whispered sighs.

Among the pines, the shadows play,
Where evening settles into gray.
A flicker shines, a candle's breath,
Alight with warmth, defying death.

The air is crisp, the night is pure,
And yet, within, we find our cure.
The quiet light, a gentle guide,
In winter's hold, hope will abide.

Each star above begins to gleam,
An echo of a distant dream.
In darkness found, a spark ignites,
A beacon bright in coldest nights.

With every heartbeat, we embrace,
The tender warmth of winter's grace.
Alight we stand, though cold surrounds,
In quiet hold, a love abounds.

Frosted Lanterns in the Stillness of Night

Beneath the moon in icy glow,
Where frost adorns the world below,
The lanterns flicker, soft and bright,
Guiding wanderers through the night.

In stillness deep, the air is clear,
The heart feels light, devoid of fear.
Each beam of light, a whispered prayer,
A promise kept in frozen air.

The world encased in crystal dreams,
Where starlit shadows softly gleam.
With every step, the night's embrace,
A dance of light, a warm embrace.

As whispers drift on frosty breath,
The chill of night defies the death.
For in this quiet, hope ignites,
Frosted lanterns, guiding lights.

In lanterns glowed, we find our way,
Through darkest hours and coldest days.
With every flicker, hope renews,
In stillness found, the heart pursues.

Light's Embrace in a Frozen Realm

In frozen realms where silence reigns,
The heart beats soft, unbroken chains.
A gentle light begins to bloom,
Breaking free from winter's gloom.

Embracing warmth, the shadows flee,
As hope awakens quietly.
Each ray a touch, a lover's call,
Binding spirits, uniting all.

Through icy paths, we wander near,
With every step, we shed our fear.
For in the dark, a flame shall rise,
Illuminating starlit skies.

With every flicker, hearts entwine,
In frozen lands, our souls align.
A tapestry of light unfolds,
In this embrace, a love retold.

Together we blaze a radiant trail,
Across the night, we will not pale.
In frozen realms, with light we claim,
A bond that sparkles, like a flame.

Warmth Under the Glistening Stars

Beneath the endless sky so wide,
Soft whispers of the night abide.
Stars above like diamonds gleam,
While dreams take flight on silver streams.

In the hush of twilight's grace,
Hearts entwine in this sacred space.
A cozy fire crackles bright,
Casting glow in the still of night.

Laughter dances on the breeze,
As shadows sway among the trees.
Bonds of love grow stronger here,
Wrapped in warmth, away from fear.

The world drifts off, so far away,
Underneath the stars that play.
Each moment cherished, never lost,
In the glimmer, we count the cost.

With every breath, the night unfolds,
An endless story yet untold.
In this warmth, we find our place,
Under the stars, in endless grace.

A Dance of Shadows and Silver Light

In the twilight's soft embrace,
Shadows weave in a haunting grace.
Silvery beams along the ground,
A secret dance, both lost and found.

The night unfolds with whispered sighs,
As moonlight flickers and softly flies.
Underneath the arching trees,
A tranquil moment, a gentle breeze.

Figures merge with shades of night,
Fleeting images, a ghostly flight.
Whirling softly in twilight's hold,
Each step a story waiting to be told.

Soft murmurs echo through the dark,
As dreams awaken to leave their mark.
In the dance of silver and shade,
The night whispers secrets that never fade.

With every turn, the heart ignites,
In this dance of shadows and lights.
Weaving moments both bright and stark,
A reminder of love in the dark.

The Hearth of Hope in a Cold World

A flicker glows in the frosty air,
A hearth of hope, tender and rare.
In the silence, our spirits rise,
Warming hearts like the brightest skies.

Outside, the world is dressed in white,
But here, we gather, igniting light.
Each spark a promise, a wish held tight,
In the coziness of our shared delight.

Voices mingle, stories weave,
In this haven, we dare believe.
Through winter's chill and biting cold,
Together, strong, our joys unfold.

The flames dance wild, casting their glow,
While outside, the winds of winter blow.
Within these walls, we find our way,
Hope's warmth shining every day.

So let the frost paint the world pale,
In our hearts, it cannot prevail.
For in this hearth, love's fire endures,
A beacon bright that forever lures.

Ethereal Flames Beneath Snowy Cover

Amidst the snow, a warmth resides,
Ethereal flames where love abides.
Under blankets of winter's grace,
A hidden glow in a quiet space.

The world outside is hushed and still,
Yet inside hearts feel the thrill.
With every flicker, spirits soar,
In the embrace of what we explore.

Glowing embers tell tales of yore,
Of laughter and dreams that we still adore.
In the chill, we find our peace,
As all our worries gently cease.

Snowflakes whisper promises sweet,
As we gather round, our lives complete.
In this moment, all feels right,
Ethereal flames, our guiding light.

With every pause, there comes a sigh,
As time drifts on, like clouds in the sky.
Beneath the snowy cover we thrive,
In the warmth of love, we feel alive.

Capturing Light in the Silent Hours

In twilight's hush, the shadows creep,
The stars awaken from their sleep.
Moonlight dances on the ground,
Whispers of night, all around.

Needles of silver pierce the dark,
Glistening softly, a tranquil spark.
Each breath of wind a gentle sigh,
As dreams take flight in the evening sky.

Moments frozen, time stands still,
The heartbeats echo, a tender thrill.
Linger here, where silence sings,
And captures light, the peace it brings.

Unseen rhythms play a tune,
Beneath the gaze of a watchful moon.
A tapestry of stillness spun,
In the quiet hours, we become one.

So let the shadows softly play,
In the silent hours, night and day.
Embrace the light, hold it tight,
For in these moments, the soul takes flight.

The Serenity of Warmth in a Frozen Dream

A blanket of white, a world asleep,
Snowflakes whisper, secrets they keep.
In the heart of winter's chill,
Warmth resides, a gentle thrill.

Softly glowing, embers glow,
Casting light on the undying snow.
Within the silence, comfort found,
Serenity wraps the frosted ground.

Beneath the icy, starry dome,
Lies a promise, a feeling of home.
Cupped in hands, the warmth we share,
Flickers of hope rise in the air.

Dreams unfurl in blankets deep,
While the world outside begins to weep.
A stillness that holds the breath of peace,
In frozen moments, all worries cease.

So let this winter's dream enfold,
A warmth that glimmers, a story told.
In each frozen flake, love's refrain,
A serenity that breaks the chain.

Fragile Flames Against the Bitter Cold

In the depths of night, embers spark,
Flickering gently, igniting the dark.
Fragile flames dance, a delicate waltz,
Defying the chill, they break down walls.

With whispered warmth in a breath so light,
They chase away shadows, banish the fright.
Each flicker a story, a heartbeat's song,
In a world so frozen, where we belong.

The bitter cold wraps the earth in white,
Yet here we gather, igniting the night.
Hands clasped together, hearts beating strong,
In the fragile flames, we find where we belong.

Courage blooms in the softest glow,
As the world outside continues to throw
Its icy grip, yet we remain bold,
Cradling warmth against the bitter cold.

So let the fire crackle and sing,
Through the darkest hours, may it bring
A union of hearts, a love untold,
In fragile flames against the bitter cold.

Dusk's Embrace and the Spark of Light

As the sun dips low, colors blend,
Dusk's embrace, a gentle friend.
Shadows stretch, the day takes flight,
In the quiet calm of fading light.

The horizon whispers secrets deep,
Inviting dreams as the world sleeps.
A spark of light ignites the night,
Guiding lost souls toward what is right.

Stars awaken, the dark unfolds,
With tales of wonder and glimmers of gold.
In dusk's embrace, we find our way,
A promise of peace to end the day.

Let the twilight cradle your fears,
And wash away the darkest years.
For in this moment, time stands still,
And the heart is freed, embraced by will.

So cherish the dusk, the rise of night,
In its soft glow, find the spark of light.
For every ending, a hopeful start,
In dusk's embrace, we mend the heart.

Drifting Light on Crystal Waters

The dawn breaks soft on shimmering waves,
Reflecting hues of gold and blue.
Gentle ripples dance like whispered grace,
Embracing dreams yet to pursue.

A sailboat glides with tranquil ease,
Painting shadows on the gleaming bay.
In this moment, worries cease,
As time drifts slowly, melts away.

The breeze carries secrets from afar,
Caught in the flow of nature's song.
Each note a promise, like a star,
Guiding hearts where they belong.

Amidst the calm, a world unfolds,
Stories hidden in every swell.
With drifting light, the heart beholds,
A sanctuary, a silent spell.

In crystal depths, reflections play,
A tapestry of fleeting light.
Each wave a canvas, night and day,
Drawing us closer to the bright.

Echoes of Home Beneath a Frozen Sky

Beneath the frost on quiet eves,
The whispers linger, soft and low.
In each heartbeat, memory weaves,
The warmth of home, a gentle glow.

The twilight paints the world in cream,
With stars that twinkle, bold and bright.
In frozen dreams, we chase the gleam,
Of love that wraps us through the night.

Footprints trace a path in snow,
Each step a tale of times once shared.
With every breath, our spirits grow,
In frosty air, no hearts are scared.

Echoes call from rooms aglow,
Where laughter spills like winter's cheer.
Underneath this sky of snow,
Home whispers softly, always near.

As dawn unfurls its icy lace,
The promise of a new day's song.
In frozen beauty, we find grace,
For in our hearts, we all belong.

The Subtle Glow of Whispered Dreams

In twilight's hush, the shadows play,
Where secrets linger, soft and bright.
A tender hope ignites the way,
Guiding souls with gentle light.

Each wish is woven, thread by thread,
In the fabric of the night's embrace.
They float like feathers, softly spread,
In this sacred, ethereal space.

The moonlight glides through branches bare,
Casting patterns on the silent ground.
In the cool air, dreams dance with care,
A symphony of whispers found.

In every heartbeat, love's soft call,
A melody that echoes clear.
With every rise and gentle fall,
Whispered dreams weave ever near.

As the dawn begins to break,
The magic fades but leaves a trace.
In our hearts, these dreams we make,
Glow forever, time can't erase.

Glowing Possibilities in a Chilly Realm

In the stillness of a frosty morn,
Where the world sparkles, crisp and bright.
Potential glows in every thorn,
Awaiting warmth, a new delight.

The icy breath on winter's cheek,
Hints at wonders yet to be.
In hushed tones, the heart may seek,
The glowing paths of destiny.

Each flake that falls, a chance anew,
A dance of fate in quiet grace.
Within the chill, the spark breaks through,
To light the dreams time can't erase.

The bitter winds may howl and bite,
Yet within us lies a steady flame.
With every step towards the light,
We find our strength, we stake our claim.

In this realm, where chill winds roam,
The heart knows warmth beyond the cold.
For in each soul lies a true home,
Glowing bright as stories unfold.

Glistening Echoes of Fire

In the night sky, embers dance,
Whispers of warmth in a glowing trance.
Flames leap high, a vivid show,
Glistening echoes of fire's flow.

The darkness fades, the shadows play,
As bright sparks chase the night away.
Each flicker tells a story old,
Of warmth and light, fierce and bold.

Among the trees, the shadows creep,
Yet the warmth around us, we will keep.
A bond ignites with every spark,
Guiding us home through the dark.

The wild winds sing their ancient tune,
As fires melt beneath the moon.
With every crackle, the heart's desire,
Awakens with glistening echoes of fire.

In the end, when silence falls,
A lasting glow in our hearts calls.
Though embers fade, memories linger,
In the warmth of fire, we find our singer.

Winter's Warm Embrace

Snowflakes dance on a gentle breeze,
A blanket white upon the trees.
In winter's chill, a warmth unfolds,
Embracing hearts with stories told.

The fireside crackles, spirits rise,
While frosty windows frame the skies.
Each sip of cocoa, sweet delight,
In winter's warm embrace, our light.

Footprints lead through a snowy field,
Where laughter's echo is revealed.
With every hug, the chill takes flight,
As hearts ignite with pure delight.

The world transformed in silver glow,
Winter whispers soft and slow.
With every flake that falls anew,
Comes warmth of love shared between two.

As days grow short and nights extend,
In this season, love transcends.
Wrapped in warmth, we stand in grace,
Forever held in winter's embrace.

Shards of Light on a Frosted Path

Morning breaks with silver beams,
Frosted paths weave through our dreams.
Shards of light on glistening snow,
Guide our steps where cold winds blow.

Each breath a cloud in the crisp air,
Nature's art, so rich and rare.
Every footprint tells a tale,
Of crisp adventures, bright and pale.

As shadows stretch and sunlight grows,
We walk where beauty freely flows.
Among the trees, a calmness speaks,
In the stillness, our spirit seeks.

The world awash in icy hues,
Whispers secrets, ancient views.
With every ounce of joy we find,
Shards of light to fill our mind.

Through winter's grace, our hearts align,
In every step, a soft design.
With shards of light, we carve our way,
On a frosted path where hopes can sway.

Ember Light on a Wintry Canvas

A canvas white sprawls far and wide,
Ember light flickers, a glowing guide.
In the stillness, the world awakes,
With shadows long that winter makes.

Crackling fires, the heart's warm cheer,
Welcoming moments, drawing near.
Each breath a warmth, a spark, a glow,
Ember light on falling snow.

Footprints marked in a gentle hush,
As time moves slow, and we feel the rush.
With every ember, a story shares,
Of love ignited in wintry layers.

Through frosted leaves and branches bare,
Whispers of warmth fill the cold air.
Painting our dreams in hues so bright,
With ember light on this canvas white.

As night descends, the world transforms,
Through glowing flames, a heart conforms.
Each flicker tells of a life profound,
In ember light, true joy is found.

Light Against a Crystal Canvas

A shimmer dances on the frost,
Glimmers bright, at what cost?
Whispers of dawn, soft and fair,
Light weaves stories in the air.

Each crystal holds a tale untold,
A glint of warmth in the cold.
Beneath the surface, life hides deep,
In frosty silence, secrets keep.

The sun spills gold on icy streams,
Reflecting hopes, igniting dreams.
Shadows stretch as moments flow,
In twilight's grace, the world will glow.

A canvas bright, of silver lace,
Nature's art in frosty space.
Light against shadows, bold and free,
A masterpiece for all to see.

Whispering Flames Upon Snow

In the quiet of the night,
Flames flicker, soft and bright.
They dance upon the blanket white,
Whispers echo, taking flight.

Each spark a story, old and new,
Drawing warmth like morning dew.
Fires cradle snowflakes' fall,
A symphony, a beckoning call.

Embers crackle, tales they spin,
In their glow, the world begins.
Frosty breath meets fiery sighs,
In this moment, magic lies.

Together they weave, worlds collide,
Within the contrast, hearts confide.
Whispering flames against the chill,
A warm embrace, winter stands still.

The Glow of Memories in Icy Silence

In icy silence, echoes breathe,
Whispers of memories beneath.
The past, a glow, both soft and bright,
Lingers on in the fading light.

Snowflakes fall like forgotten dreams,
Each one holds a tale, it seems.
Beneath the surface, warmth resides,
In frozen realms where time abides.

Frosted windows, shades of gray,
Frame the glow of yesterday.
With each blink, the world unfolds,
A tapestry of dreams retold.

Stillness deep as twilight's reach,
In its calm, no need for speech.
The icy silence, a gentle friend,
Where every memory finds its end.

Elysium Beneath the Winter's Breath

Underneath winter's aching breath,
Lies a realm of dreams and death.
Elysium waits, a hidden place,
Where time and frost interlace.

In glistening white, the world transforms,
A sacred space where silence warms.
The breath of snow in twilight glows,
Breeding magic in soft flows.

Beneath the chill, life whispers low,
In every drift, in every snow.
Hidden wonders, softly tread,
Elysium blooms where souls are led.

With each step upon the crystalline ground,
Memories of warmth and love abound.
In this gentle hush, hearts align,
Winter's breath becomes divine.

Aurora of Flames in Winter's Hold

In the sky, the colors dance,
Flickers of life in winter's trance.
Crimson and gold, a warming glow,
Against the chill, they steal the show.

Whispers of warmth in icy air,
Nature's beauty beyond compare.
Each spark ignites a frozen dream,
Embers burning, a vibrant theme.

Shadows stretch across the ground,
Silent stories, then surround.
Hues of fire, against the white,
A testament of hope and light.

Beneath the veil of the night's cold kiss,
Lies a realm wrapped in bliss.
The aurora weaves its magic thread,
Softly guiding those who tread.

As winter bows to the flames' embrace,
Life's resurgence finds its place.
In the frosty grip, warmth unfolds,
A symphony of colors bold.

Echoes of Light in the Frosted Silence

In the stillness, whispers flow,
Through the frost, a gentle glow.
Echoes of light across the land,
Their soft caress, a tender hand.

Silent snowflakes dance and twirl,
In the night, they softly swirl.
Each flake bears a story old,
Of winter's magic, silent and cold.

Beneath the stars, the shadows play,
As dawn approaches, night turns gray.
The echoes linger, sweet and true,
Painting the world in softest hue.

Through the hush, a warmth can build,
In the heart, a space is filled.
Light emerges from deep inside,
Breaking through, like a rising tide.

As silence reigns, we find our voice,
In the stillness, we rejoice.
Echoes of light in every heart,
A sacred bond, we'll never part.

A Glowing Heart in the Heart of Winter

Within the frost, a flame ignites,
A glowing heart, through winter nights.
Wrapped in layers, warmth we seek,
In the dark, our spirits speak.

Snowflakes twinkle, stars above,
Blanketing earth with whispers of love.
Each breath a cloud in the chill,
A promise made, a heart to fill.

Amidst the cold, a spark of cheer,
Friendship blooms, drawing near.
Laughter echoes through the pale,
In winter's grip, we will prevail.

With cozy moments, time stands still,
In the heart, a gentle thrill.
Together, we face the bitter wind,
In our warmth, the joy rescinds.

As seasons shift and days grow bright,
The glowing heart shines in the night.
Winter fades, but love remains,
In every heart, a warmth sustains.

Illuminating the Depth of Cold Nights

In the depths where shadows creep,
A light ignites, no longer sleep.
Flickering flames break the night,
Illuminating with pure delight.

In the stillness, a glow appears,
Whispered hopes mixed with fears.
Each flicker tells a sacred tale,
Of resilience against the pale.

Through the crackling of the fire,
We find the warmth that fuels desire.
In each ember, dreams take flight,
Claiming back the lost delight.

The world outside is crisp and stark,
Yet here, we light a vibrant spark.
In togetherness, we stand as one,
Facing the chill, 'til night is done.

As dawn breaks through the lingering cold,
The stories of warmth shall be retold.
Illuminated hearts will shine bright,
Guiding us forth into the light.

Glimmering Shadows on Ice

Beneath the moonlit sky so wide,
The shadows dance, they glide with pride.
Each flicker tells a tale of night,
In glimmering hues, a frozen light.

The surface shines with silver gleam,
While whispers weave through dreams that seem.
Step softly on this crystal floor,
Where time stands still, forevermore.

Each crack a song, each breath a sigh,
In icy realms where secrets lie.
The stars above like diamonds cast,
In glimmering shadows, moments vast.

With every step, a story flows,
In chilling air where friendship grows.
The world transforms, a canvas clear,
Glimmering shadows draw us near.

So linger long where night unfolds,
In frozen whispers, warmth consoled.
Together in this sparkling trance,
We find our hearts in icy dance.

The Hearth's Whispering Light

In corners bright, where embers glow,
The heart finds peace that we all know.
A hearth's embrace, warm and inviting,
With whispers soft, gently igniting.

The crackling fire tells tales of old,
Of laughter shared and dreams retold.
The light flickers, shadows sway,
In this cozy nook, night turns to day.

Memories linger, rich and sweet,
As we gather 'round, our hearts in beat.
The hearth reflects in every face,
A tapestry of love and grace.

So let the warmth envelop all,
The hearth's whisper, a soothing call.
In togetherness, let joy ignite,
With every spark, our souls take flight.

As stories blend, the long hours wane,
In the hearth's light, we lose all pain.
A simple moment, cherished and right,
Forever held in the whispering light.

Sparkling Silence of December

In silence deep, the snowflakes fall,
December whispers, a magic call.
Each crystal gleam, a breath of freeze,
Sparkling softly on the trees.

The world is wrapped in quiet grace,
Each flurry finds its perfect place.
A moment still, beneath the sky,
Where dreams take flight and spirits fly.

The crisp air sings a winter's tune,
As stars emerge, a silvery boon.
The silence speaks, profound and wide,
In December's hold, our hearts abide.

With twinkling lights on every block,
Advent calendars tick and clock.
Each day unpacks a gift to share,
In sparkling silence, love and care.

So let us breathe this winter peace,
And find our hurried thoughts a cease.
In every flake, a story bright,
In sparkling silence, pure delight.

Illumination in a Frozen Breath

As dawn breaks forth with colors rare,
In frozen breath, we find the air.
Each moment sparkles, crisp and clear,
Illumination, winter's cheer.

The frosted branches glimmer bright,
Each crystal shard catches the light.
In every corner, magic stirs,
With whispers soft, the silence purrs.

We tread on paths where frost has laid,
A frozen world, a silent parade.
The skies above, a canvas spun,
Each breath we take, a morning run.

Gathered near, we share our warmth,
In frozen breath, a common charm.
Illumination in every glance,
A magic spell of winter's dance.

So let us pause and hold this dream,
In frozen whispers, time's gentle stream.
Each heartbeat echoes, sweet and strong,
Illumination where we belong.

The Chilly Dance of Shimmering Flames

In the frigid air they sway,
Bright hues in the night play,
Glistening hearts in winter's bite,
A dance of warmth in cold's light.

Whispers rise in flickers bold,
Stories of warmth, quietly told,
Around the fire, we take our stand,
Feeling pulses in the frosty land.

Embers glow like stars above,
Casting shadows, dreams we love,
With every spark a wish we send,
In this chilly magic, hearts we'll mend.

As the night deepens its hue,
The flickering light finds me and you,
Shimmering flames, our spirits dance,
In the glow, we find romance.

So let the chilly breezes howl,
In the warmth of fire, we shall prowl,
For in the dance of blazing dreams,
Life is more than what it seems.

Sapphire Nights and Golden Glows

Underneath the sapphire skies,
Golden rays begin to rise,
Whispers soft from twilight's breath,
Heralding the night of death.

Stars come forth, in bold array,
Painting visions where we play,
Gold and blue in endless flight,
Chasing shadows, holding light.

Laughter mingles with the breeze,
Carried sweet through swaying trees,
In this world of deep delight,
We bask in the depth of night.

Moments flicker, memories blend,
In the glow where spirits mend,
Sapphire dreams, golden hopes,
In the dark, our love elopes.

Together we embrace the glow,
Heartbeats echo, steady flow,
In the dance of night so bright,
Sapphire dreams take fearless flight.

Ghostly Frost with a Tender Flicker

Ghostly frost adorns the trees,
Whispers linger on the breeze,
Tender flickers chase the chill,
Where the world is hushed and still.

Silvery lights through shadows gleam,
In this frost, we dare to dream,
Touching hearts with every spark,
Illuminating winter's dark.

With every breath, the air does freeze,
Yet warmth surrounds in memories,
Flickering flames hold us tight,
In the heart of the frigid night.

Through the frost, our laughter flows,
As the flicker gently glows,
In this moment, time stands still,
Embracing warmth against the chill.

Let the frost become our muse,
With flickered lights, we cannot lose,
In this ghostly, tender space,
We'll find our joy, a warm embrace.

Hearthside Reflections in the Winter Dark

Hearthside warmth, a glowing sight,
Reflections dance in amber light,
Winter dark shrouds the night,
Yet here, we find our hearts' delight.

Crackling wood, a gentle song,
Where stories told echo long,
With every tale, the shadows blend,
Creating bonds that never end.

Outside, the world is crisp and cold,
Inside, the hearth's embrace we hold,
In the glow, our worries cease,
Wrapped in laughter, love, and peace.

As the night wraps around our dreams,
Fireside warmth, a soft moonbeams,
Together here, hand in hand tight,
We weave our stories through the night.

So let the winter howl and roar,
For here beside the hearth we soar,
In the dance of shadows cast,
We'll cherish moments that hold fast.

Gentle Glow in a Bitter Wind

The sun dips low, a shy retreat,
Casting warmth on frozen streets.
Whispers of light, so soft and bright,
Embracing all in fading night.

A breeze that bites, yet holds a care,
Gentle glow, a fleeting stare.
Remaining hope in shadows cast,
A tender moment, a spell to last.

Through icy branches, soft winds weave,
Stories told to those who believe.
A flicker shines amidst the gray,
A gentle glow to guide the way.

In bitter wind, we find our call,
Against the chill, we cannot fall.
Together strong, we face the dusk,
In gentle light, we place our trust.

Each breath we take, a fragile song,
In this still place, we feel we belong.
Wrapped in warmth, though cold it seems,
A gentle glow, the heart still dreams.

Shooting Sparks on a Winter's Morn

Morning breaks with crisp delight,
Stars dissolve in the fading night.
Shooting sparks, the sky ignites,
Winter whispers of new heights.

Frosted air, a playful tease,
Trees adorned with sparkling freeze.
Sunrise dances on snowy peaks,
Nature's voice, it softly speaks.

Footprints trace a silent path,
In the calm, we share a laugh.
Every breath a clouded sigh,
Underneath the vast, blue sky.

Promises held in frosty breath,
Hope ignites where there is death.
On this morn, the world awakes,
Shooting sparks, the heart partakes.

Through the chill, we find the flame,
Winter's love, a daring game.
In the light of dawn's embrace,
Shooting sparks, we find our place.

The Warmth of Solitude Under Ice

In the silence, shadows grow,
Underneath a sheet of snow.
The world, it fades, but hearts remain,
In solitude, we feel no pain.

Glimmers of warmth in winter's hold,
Stories whispered, yet untold.
A single flame, a quiet spark,
Guides us gently through the dark.

The ice may cradle, but so does peace,
In stillness large, all troubles cease.
Wrapped in thoughts like softest fleece,
The warmth of solitude, our release.

Beneath the frost, a life does bloom,
In every heart, a hidden room.
Solitude sings a haunting tune,
Beneath the watchful, cold moon.

In chilly nights, our spirits rise,
Finding light in starry skies.
With every breath, a gift we find,
The warmth of solitude, intertwined.

Sparkling Gold in Silver Frost

Morning breaks with jeweled light,
Frosty fields, a dazzling sight.
Sparkling gold on winter's lace,
Nature's dance, a soft embrace.

Each crystal glows, a fleeting glance,
In this frost, we take our chance.
Moments captured, time on hold,
Stories whispered, brave and bold.

The sun ascends, the world aglow,
In silver frost, the shadows flow.
Every breath a painted hue,
Sparkling gold, the day feels new.

Through every flake that drifts and sways,
A symphony in cold displays.
With laughter shared, we twirl and spin,
Against the chill, warmth lies within.

In winter's grasp, we find our cheer,
With sparkling dreams that bring us near.
Gold in silver, a sight to boast,
Warming hearts, this season's toast.

Twilight's Embrace with a Glowing Heart

As daylight fades, the shadows creep,
A hush envelops, the world asleep.
Stars awaken, shimmering bright,
In twilight's arms, we find our light.

Whispers of dusk in the gentle breeze,
Kiss of the night among the trees.
Crickets sing their evening song,
In twilight's embrace, we all belong.

The sky ignites in hues of gold,
Stories of dreams waiting to be told.
Gentle warmth in the cooling air,
Twilight's glow, a tender prayer.

Silhouettes dance as colors blend,
In this soft moment, hearts transcend.
Memories linger in the fading light,
A glowing heart in the silent night.

With every sigh, the day departs,
Leaving us with aglowing hearts.
In twilight's closeness, time stands still,
Our spirits soar, and love will fill.

Frosty Breath in Golden Light

Morning breaks with a shimmering sight,
Breath of frost in the golden light.
A canvas painted by winter's hand,
Nature's beauty, serene and grand.

Trees adorned with glistening lace,
In each sparkle, a quiet grace.
Footsteps crunch on the icy ground,
In this stillness, magic is found.

Sunrise spills over hills so steep,
While the world in silence gently sleeps.
Bated breath in the brightening hue,
Frosty whispers, so soft and true.

Chill in the air, yet warmth inside,
Wrapped in layers, we choose to bide.
The beauty here transcends mere sight,
Frosty breath in the golden light.

Every corner, a world anew,
Timeless wonder in every view.
In the frost, our spirits ignite,
Chasing dreams in the morning light.

Ember Reflections on Cold Surfaces

In the hearth, the embers glow,
Casting warmth in the evening's flow.
Reflections dance on cold, sleek panes,
Stories told in flickering flames.

Outside, the winter's breath is stark,
Yet inside, we gather, hearts spark.
Whispers of stories, soft and clear,
In embered light, we draw near.

Each flame a memory, bright and bold,
Of laughter shared, of love untold.
While the world outside may freeze,
Here we find our hearts at ease.

The night unfolds with a gentle sigh,
As embers fade, we wonder why.
Yet in our dreams, the warmth remains,
Reflections held in the glowing flames.

From fleeting light, we learn to see,
The beauty found in you and me.
In every ember, hope's embrace,
Cold surfaces warm with love's grace.

Soft Flickers in the Frozen Stillness

Evening settles, a quiet spell,
Whispers of winter, soft and swell.
In frozen stillness, magic stirs,
With soft flickers, the heart concurs.

Lights twinkle in the distant trees,
Carried gently by the frosty breeze.
Each glimmer a wish, a silent prayer,
A promise held in the frigid air.

The night unveils its shimmering gown,
A blanket of silver, a delicate crown.
All around, the world aglow,
In soft flickers, our spirits flow.

Through the stillness, dreams take flight,
Guided by stars in the velvety night.
In this moment, we lose our fear,
Soft flickers draw our loved ones near.

Embracing shadows, we dance and sway,
In frozen stillness, we find our way.
With hearts alight, we forge ahead,
Soft flickers of love, where dreams are bred.

Warming the Chill in the Air

In the hearth, a glow does rise,
Soft warmth seen in amber skies.
Snowflakes fall with gentle grace,
Embraced by warmth, a loving space.

Fires crackle, shadows play,
Homes alight, chasing gray.
Laughter echoes through the night,
As hearts entwine in shared delight.

Outside, the frost bites cold,
But inside, stories unfold.
Toast the night with joy and cheer,
For warmth resides when loved ones near.

Candles flicker, soft and bright,
Hope ignites, hearts take flight.
Through winter's chill, we'll find our way,
In warmth and love, we shall stay.

And though the cold may linger long,
The warmth of souls will keep us strong.
Side by side, throughout the year,
We cherish love that conquers fear.

Luminous Visions of a Frosty Eve

Upon the ground, a blanket white,
Stars above, a sparkling sight.
Moonlight dances, shadows play,
Guiding dreams, the gentle sway.

Whispers of winter, soft and clear,
Echo through the frosty sphere.
Each breath forms a cloud so sweet,
As magic weaves beneath our feet.

Icicles hang like crystal art,
Nature's canvas, a work of heart.
Luminous visions fill the night,
In frozen stillness, pure delight.

The world transformed, a glistening show,
With every step, the softness glows.
In the chill, we find our peace,
A tranquil night that will not cease.

Through the frosty veil, we see,
Luminous dreams await you and me.
In winter's kiss, serenity,
Together, we'll embrace the mystery.

The Dance of Flame and Ice

Flickering flames in the dark,
A warm embrace, a vibrant spark.
Outside, the world is cold and stark,
Inside, we find our joyful mark.

Ice crystals twinkle, shimmering bright,
While embers glow with a gentle light.
Heat meets frost, a wondrous dance,
In harmony, we take our chance.

Spirits rise with every breath,
In this balance of life and death.
With every flicker, shadows play,
As night transforms into the day.

The fire crackles, the ice does gleam,
Together they weave a vibrant dream.
A tapestry of warmth and chill,
In this moment, we feel the thrill.

And when the dawn begins to break,
The remnants of night softly shake.
Flame and ice, forever entwined,
In every heart, their strength combined.

Radiance Amidst the Chill

Through winter's breath, we find a glow,
A radiant warmth in the falling snow.
With every flake, a wonder unveils,
In silence, the beauty never fails.

Softly shining, the stars above,
Whispering tales of warmth and love.
In the dark, a spark ignites,
Shining brightly on frosty nights.

Together we gather, hearts aligned,
In the chill, our spirits blind.
Fires burn bright, casting light,
Radiance flowing, pure delight.

As the winds sing their cold refrain,
We find comfort amidst the pain.
Wrapped in layers, held so tight,
Together, we greet the starry night.

So let the chill wrap around us here,
In love's embrace, we'll persevere.
For in our hearts, we carry the fire,
Radiance brightens every desire.

Flickers of Joy in a Glacial Realm

In stillness deep where cold winds sigh,
Small lights emerge, a hopeful cry.
Crystals glint with stories untold,
Life springs forth from the shards of cold.

A flicker here, a dance so bright,
Amidst the white, a pulse of light.
Snowflakes twirl in a joyful tease,
Nature's rhythm, a heart at ease.

Beneath the sky, so vast and gray,
Glimmers flicker, lead hearts astray.
Moments blend like hues in a dream,
In frozen realms, they leap and gleam.

The chill bites sharp, yet warmth resides,
In fleeting sparks where wonder glides.
Each breath a testament to the glow,
That thrives in places where few dare go.

In the glacial realm where shadows play,
Joy finds its voice, come what may.
Each flicker, a reminder, profound,
That warmth can blossom in frosty ground.

Fragments of Warmth in a Frozen Landscape

Amidst the frost where silence reigns,
Tiny embers break the chains.
Shimmering softly like stars on ice,
Each fragment whispers, a sweet device.

In the heart of winter's icy grip,
Heat springs forth, a gentle sip.
Scattered rays on snowflakes rest,
Comfort found in nature's chest.

Footprints trace where warmth survives,
In the depths where passion thrives.
Here, every breath draws worlds anew,
In frozen lands, hope finds its view.

Cold winds carry a tender hue,
Of love and laughter breaking through.
In crystal gardens, dreams are sown,
A tapestry of warmth alone.

Each fragment glows with stories bright,
Illuminating the dark of night.
In frozen landscapes, love ignites,
A dance of warmth in winter's bites.

A Whisper of Light in the Arctics

In the Arctic where shadows reign,
A whisper of light touches the plain.
Faintly glowing on the tundra wide,
A gentle spark where hopes abide.

Calm descends as night unfolds,
Soft glimmers tell the stories told.
Each flicker holds a world inside,
In silence deep, our dreams collide.

Beneath the stars, so vast and bright,
Whispers entwine with the frosty night.
The dance of auroras, soft and free,
A symphony of light, a reverie.

Cold and clear, the air hangs tight,
Yet warmth exudes from the heart of night.
Hope wanders where the cold winds blow,
A whisper of love in the frosty glow.

In Arctic realms, where few have tread,
The light of dreams gently spread.
Each whisper carries a tranquil grace,
Embracing the chill in nature's embrace.

Celestial Flames on a Frosty Canvas

On a canvas white, celestial flames,
Dance with shadows, play their games.
Fireflies weave through the starry night,
Illuminating paths of pure delight.

With every flicker, the dark gives way,
To vibrant hues in a frosty play.
Warmth ignites in the breath of cold,
A tapestry of colors bold.

As winter sleeps, dreams start to bloom,
In fiery sparks, they carve the gloom.
A radiant burst amidst the chill,
Nature's magic, a heart to fill.

In this frozen world of silence deep,
Celestial flames awaken sleep.
Each spark a tale of love and cheer,
Guiding souls with light sincere.

On frosty canvases, hope is spun,
Under the gaze of a setting sun.
Celestial flames, through the night they rise,
Painting warmth in the winter skies.

The Soft Glow of Winter's Breath

Winter whispers through the trees,
A blanket white, so soft, so deep.
Stars twinkle gently in the night,
As cold winds sing and shadows creep.

The moonlight dances on the snow,
Casting dreams in silvery hues.
Each breath a cloud, each step a tune,
In this realm where silence woos.

A frosty breath upon my cheek,
Nature's heart beats slow and low.
In this stillness, time stands still,
As winter's magic starts to flow.

Glistening trees like crystal spires,
Whisper secrets that winter keeps.
The world adorned in icy lace,
While every sound in slumber sleeps.

So let us savor this cold night,
Wrapped in warmth, our spirits bright.
For in the soft glow of winter's breath,
We find solace, love, and light.

Echoes of Light in the Frozen Woods

Amidst the trees where shadows fall,
A glow emerges from the frost.
The whispers of the willows call,
In icy beauty, none are lost.

Glimmers dance on frozen streams,
Reflecting all that nature hides.
The echoes of our childhood dreams,
In winter's woods, the heart abides.

Footsteps soft on crisp, white ground,
Each crunch a note in winter's song.
Amongst the pines, peace can be found,
In this realm where we belong.

The light cascades, a gentle stream,
Through branches bare, revealing grace.
In every glimmer, hope may beam,
And time stands still in its embrace.

So wander here, let worries cease,
Underneath the starry skies.
In frozen woods, we find our peace,
With echoes of light as our guide.

A Glacial Night's Warm Embrace

The world is wrapped in quiet blue,
A glacial night, serene and bright.
In this embrace, my thoughts run true,
Underneath the silver light.

Frosty air against my skin,
Each breath a sparkle, crisp and clear.
In this abyss where dreams begin,
I find the warmth of love held dear.

Stars like diamonds, bold and brave,
Shimmering in the vast expanse.
In their glow, my spirit's saved,
Captured in this winter's dance.

With every heartbeat, time slows down,
In glacial tranquility, we glide.
The earth adorned with frosty crown,
Where warmth and winter can collide.

So hold me close, 'neath starry skies,
As winter weaves its gentle thread.
In this embrace, our spirits rise,
And fears dissolve, their power shed.

Ethereal Light on Frostbitten Ground

Ethereal light bathes the cold,
In shades of blue and silver sheen.
Each step across the frostbitten fold,
Reveals a beauty, soft and keen.

Underneath the velvet sky,
The earth lies wrapped in dreams of white.
As winter's breath begins to sigh,
We dance beneath the pale moonlight.

Trees stand tall, their branches bare,
A testament to nature's reign.
In this moment, free from care,
Where joy and solitude remain.

With every flicker, shadows play,
On glistening fields of untouched snow.
In silence, we can find our way,
Through winter's realm, our spirits flow.

So let us greet the night with grace,
And wander through this frosted dream.
For in the light that time cannot erase,
We find the warmth in winter's gleam.

Luminous Echoes of a Winter's Night

Under the pale moonlight's grace,
Whispers of night begin to trace.
Stars dance in the frozen air,
Dreams linger softly everywhere.

A blanket of snow lays so bright,
Each flake a gleam against the night.
Footsteps crunch on the silent ground,
Winter's lullaby is all around.

The trees stand tall, their branches bare,
Echoing secrets, a frozen stare.
In this stillness, hearts ignite,
Luminous echoes chase away fright.

Breath makes clouds in the frosty air,
Nature's wonder, a tranquil affair.
The night unfolds, a magic scene,
In winter's embrace, all feels serene.

With every sigh, and every glance,
The shadows begin to dance and prance.
In the quiet, we find our way,
Luminous echoes guide the day.

The Flicker That Defies the Chill

Amidst the frost, a flame glows bright,
A candle's warmth, an endless fight.
Each flicker tells a tale untold,
Defying cold, as spirits unfold.

The hearth crackles, embers fly,
Puzzles of warmth beneath a sky.
Gathering near, we share our dreams,
In the glow, hope brightly beams.

Soft shadows stretch upon the wall,
Echoing laughter, the sweetest call.
Together we stand, hand in hand,
Against the chill, we take a stand.

The night wraps us in its icy cloak,
Yet in this warmth, the heart awoke.
With every flicker, fears subside,
In the glow, our souls collide.

The winter winds may howl and scream,
But we find peace in every beam.
A flicker that burns through the night,
Defying chill with pure delight.

Shadows of Warmth in Icy Reflections

In mirrored ponds where stillness thrives,
Shadows of warmth, where hope survives.
Icy whispers grace the frozen shore,
Each moment a memory to restore.

Reflections dance in the evening haze,
A world transformed in a chill's embrace.
With every ripple, we find release,
From winter's grip, a moment of peace.

Branches glisten with crystal tears,
Offering solace to fading fears.
We gather close, our hearts entwined,
In these shadows, love's light we find.

The frost may bite, but warmth we share,
In icy reflections, the world feels rare.
Together we weave memories bright,
Shadows of warmth in the winter night.

As stars emerge from the canvas dark,
Laughter ignites a glowing spark.
In this cold, our spirits take flight,
Shadows of warmth in the gentle night.

Serene Glow in the Frostbitten Air

The dawn arrives with a gentle glow,
Touching the frosted earth below.
Each breath a visible dance of light,
In the stillness, all feels right.

A world draped in white, pure and vast,
Memories of summer fading fast.
Yet in the cold, a warmth we find,
Serene moments gently intertwined.

The sun peeks through with a shy embrace,
Illuminating every place.
With every ray, shadows retreat,
Frostbitten air, a soothing sheet.

Nature listens, a hushed reply,
As winter's whispers drift and sigh.
In this peace, hearts open wide,
In the serene glow, we all confide.

With every season's soft caress,
We learn to cherish, to love, to bless.
In the frost, in the quiet air,
A serene glow is always there.

Whispers of Winter Glow

In the stillness of the night,
Whispers of winter softly glide,
Snowflakes dance in silver light,
As the world begins to hide.

Frosted branches, glistening bright,
Crisp air wraps around like silk,
Nature's breath, a frosty sight,
Wrapped in dreams as warm as milk.

Silent echoes fill the air,
As every shadow takes its form,
Winter's chill, a gentle care,
In the quiet, spirits warm.

With each step, a soft crunch sound,
In this wonderland we roam,
Footprints trace where love is found,
In this cold, our hearts call home.

Stars above like diamonds twinkling,
Over blankets white they lay,
Winter's song, a sweet sprinkling,
Guiding us through the sleigh.

Chilled Dreams in Amber Light

In the amber glow of dusk,
Chilled dreams swirl like autumn leaves,
Whispered thoughts in twilight's husk,
As the heart secretly grieves.

Beneath the veil of evening's air,
Frosty whispers tiptoe in,
Twilight's charm begins to share,
Soft warmth where shadows have been.

Time slows down, a gentle pause,
As amber hues hold tight and near,
In the stillness, beauty draws,
Memories wrapped, crystal clear.

Dreams take flight on frosty wings,
Hopes ignited in the dark,
Echoes vibrant, softly sings,
While the world ignites its spark.

In this realm of chilled delight,
Wonders weave through dusky trails,
As stars above begin to light,
Guiding hearts where love prevails.

A Flame Amidst the Chill

By the hearth where embers glow,
A flame dances, warm and bright,
Against the chill, it sways and flows,
Crafting shadows in the night.

Winter winds outside may howl,
But here, a sanctuary stands,
In its warmth, our hopes we prowl,
Finding solace in soft hands.

Flickering light, a tender grace,
Ignites the dark with golden hues,
In this small, enchanted space,
Love's reflections gently fuse.

Stories shared, laughter glows,
In this haven, time stands still,
As the firelight softly shows,
The warmth of hearts, a powerful thrill.

Even as the frost bites deep,
In this moment, we are whole,
A flame that never will seep,
Stays a light within the soul.

Radiance in the Frosted Night

Underneath a silver sky,
Radiance dances, pure and bright,
Frosted whispers, hearts comply,
Wrapped in wonders of the night.

Moonlight spills on snow-kissed ground,
Making magic with each step,
Nature's beauty all around,
In its arms, we softly wept.

Stars like diamonds play their role,
Shimmering in the chilly air,
Every glimmer, a piece of soul,
Leading us beyond despair.

In this realm, where dreams awake,
Mysteries unfold and unwind,
In the night, our hearts will stake,
A claim to love, forever kind.

Embrace the peace, let spirits soar,
In the frost, find warmth within,
Radiance whispers evermore,
As the night begins to thin.

Whispers in the Winter Glow

In the stillness, soft winds play,
Whispers echo, night turns to day.
Snowflakes dance on silent ground,
Magic lingers, peace is found.

Frosty breath upon the air,
Nature's beauty, pure and rare.
Moonlight glimmers on the hills,
Chilling silence, heart it fills.

Branches bow with frosty lace,
In this winter's warm embrace.
Candles flicker, glows so bright,
Guiding dreams through starry night.

Footsteps crunch on fresh white snow,
Finding paths where dreams can flow.
Voices blend, a quiet song,
In this moment, we belong.

A blanket's warmth against the cold,
In whispers, secrets are foretold.
Under stars, our wishes fly,
In winter's glow, we'll never die.

Shadows of the Illuminated Night

Beneath the veil of starlit skies,
Whispers linger, shadows rise.
Fancy dances in the glow,
Fleeting moments softly flow.

Moonbeams drip on silent streams,
Carrying the weight of dreams.
Every shadow tells a tale,
Mysteries that softly trail.

Lanterns flicker, secrets blend,
In darkness, worlds extend.
Figures move with gentle grace,
Stories hidden in each face.

Echoes bounce off cobblestones,
Underneath the silver tones.
Nighttime wraps us in its shawl,
Embracing every whispered call.

Journeys sparked by quiet sights,
In the shadows of the nights.
Guided by a guiding light,
Together, we'll chase the night.

Frost-Kissed Flames

Embers glow in winter's breath,
Dancing flames defy the death.
Frosty air, the warmth we crave,
Within the fire, memories save.

Crackle, pop, the wood ignites,
Chasing shadows through the nights.
Whispers float on heated air,
Carried softly, free of care.

All around, the world is still,
Hearts ignited, laughter spills.
Fireside tales spun with delight,
Warmth embraces, holding tight.

Through the window, frost does weave,
Magic moments we believe.
Eyes reflect the dancing light,
In our hearts, the fire's bright.

Frost-kissed flames, a true embrace,
In each flicker, love we trace.
Winter's chill will fade away,
As warm embers lead the way.

Glimmering Dreams on Icy Windows

Glimmers dance on icy panes,
Beauty formed from winter's chains.
Each frost flower tells its tale,
Whispers float upon the gale.

Gentle patterns, nature's art,
Capture dreams that fill the heart.
As sunlight breaks the cold embrace,
Magic lingers, time won't race.

Windows dressed in icy lace,
Reflective dreams, a timeless space.
Figures lost in frozen frames,
In their stillness, hope remains.

Fingers trace along the glass,
Following where memories pass.
In the chill, we find the glow,
Glimmering dreams, whispers flow.

As daylight spills upon the earth,
Awakening the season's mirth.
Through frosted glass, we make our plans,
In every dream, the heart expands.

Warmth Beneath a Crystal Canopy

Underneath the starry glow,
A tranquil hush, a soft white flow.
The world adorned, a gleaming sight,
Whispers of warmth in the cold of night.

Branches draped in winter lace,
Each twinkle holds a timeless grace.
Breath of frost, a fleeting kiss,
In this serene, enchanted bliss.

Gentle sighs from the cosmic dome,
Nestled here, we find our home.
In the silence, dreams take flight,
Beneath the crystal sky so bright.

Embers glow in the heart's retreat,
Echoes of warmth in the frosty beat.
In every flake, a story spun,
Under this canopy, we're as one.

Holding hands, we brave the chill,
Finding solace, hearts to fill.
With whispers shared, our spirits rise,
Beneath the stars, love never dies.

Embrace of a Winter's Flame

Fires crackle in the night,
Casting shadows, warm and bright.
Winter's chill meets glowing light,
In this cozy, sweet delight.

The air is crisp, the world is still,
Yet hearts are warm, and spirits thrill.
With every spark, a story spun,
Embracing love until the dawn.

Snowflakes dance, a soft ballet,
While we gather, come what may.
In the glow of the flickering flames,
We share our hopes, our dreams, our names.

Laughter mingles with the smoke,
In this warmth, the silence broke.
With every sip of spiced delight,
We savor moments, sweet and bright.

As the night wraps 'round us tight,
In winter's hold, we find our light.
An embrace that time can't sever,
Finding warmth in this forever.

Frosty Gleams and Gentle Flames

Frosty gleams on windowpanes,
Nature's art in icy chains.
Outside, the world a sparkling gem,
Inside, warmth like a sacred hymn.

Gentle flames in the hearth's embrace,
Dancing shadows, a soft lace.
With every flicker, spirits rise,
Kindled warmth beneath dark skies.

Sipping cocoa, laughter shared,
In golden light, we feel prepared.
The chill outside, a distant thought,
In this haven, joy is sought.

The stars above in silence gleam,
While we bask in our winter dream.
With hearts aglow and eyes that gleam,
Together we weave our heartfelt theme.

Lost in moments, time stands still,
In frosty air and warmth, we thrill.
With gentle flames and frosty gleams,
We find our way through tangled dreams.

The Radiant Chill of Twilight

Twilight creeps with radiant chill,
Painting skies, the night distill.
A canvas brushed with violet hue,
Whispers of magic, fresh and new.

The sun dips low, a soft goodbye,
As stars awaken in the sky.
In the breather of twilight's grace,
We gather 'round, our sacred space.

Shadows stretch and gently creep,
In this moment, silence deep.
The world transformed, a dreamlike state,
Each heartbeat, a pulse of fate.

Crisp air tinged with stories told,
In the twilight, hearts unfold.
A radiant chill, a warm embrace,
Held together in time and space.

As night descends with magic spun,
We cherish moments, two as one.
In twilight's glow, let worries cease,
Wrapped in laughter, we find peace.

Twilight's Soft Warmth

As day fades into night, so bright,
The sky blushes with hues of light.
Whispers of dusk in the gentle air,
Embrace the quiet, all cares laid bare.

A moment caught in the fading glow,
Where dreams awaken, softly flow.
Stars peek out, shy and bold,
Nature's story quietly told.

The horizon melts in shades of rose,
In twilight's warmth, the heart knows.
Time stands still for a brief sigh,
Underneath the painted sky.

Fireflies dance in the cooling breeze,
Nature's rhythm puts the mind at ease.
As the world settles into its rest,
In twilight's arms, we find our best.

Come, let us linger in this divine,
Where calm and peace intertwine.
With every heartbeat, every glance,
In twilight's soft embrace, we dance.

Flickering Hope in a Frigid World

In winter's grasp, the world turns cold,
Yet flickers of warmth, brave and bold.
Amidst the snow, a candle's glow,
A beacon of hope in the frigid flow.

Each flame a story, a dream to share,
Of love and laughter that linger there.
In frozen silence, whispers ignite,
A promise of warmth in the darkest night.

Through barren branches, the winds do sigh,
Yet deep within, the embers lie.
Time may challenge, but hearts hold tight,
To the flickering hope in the fading light.

Together we gather, in this cold place,
Finding warmth in each other's embrace.
Through frostbitten paths, we bravely tread,
With flickering hope, our spirits are fed.

In a world so frigid, we stand as one,
Holding onto dreams until the day is done.
When spring arrives in a burst of gold,
Flickering hope will turn to bold.

Beneath the Icy Starlit Sky

Beneath a blanket of shimmering night,
Stars glimmer softly, a welcome sight.
The world is still, wrapped in quiet dreams,
Whispers of winter, where starlight gleams.

Each twinkle a tale of ages past,
Connecting hearts, memories cast.
In the grasp of cold, warmth hints nearby,
A promise woven, beneath the sky.

The moon hangs low, a guardian bright,
Watching over through the endless night.
In this tranquility, all seems right,
Beneath the icy starlit light.

In every flake, a wonder unfolds,
Nature's artistry, pure as gold.
With every breath, we ponder and sigh,
The magic surrounding, beneath the sky.

Let us embrace the chill of the air,
In frozen beauty, find warmth to share.
With stars as our guide, we will not part,
For beneath this sky, we warm each heart.

Shadows of Warmth in a Bitter World

In corners dark, where shadows creep,
A flicker of warmth awakens deep.
Even in bitterness, love can bloom,
Casting out echoes, dispelling gloom.

Through trials faced, our spirits rise,
In the coldest moments, we find the prize.
Hands held tight, through storms we roam,
In shadows of warmth, we find our home.

A smile exchanged in a passing glance,
In the harshest world, sparks still dance.
Every heart carries its own light,
Illuminating paths in the darkest night.

Though winds may howl, and ice may sting,
In unity, we create everything.
Together we thrive, despite the strife,
Shadows of warmth, the pulse of life.

So let us gather, in hope and grace,
Creating warmth in this bitter place.
For together we stand, through challenges swirled,
In shadows of warmth, we heal the world.

Snowflakes and Ember Dreams

Snowflakes dance on silent air,
Each one unique, a gem so rare.
They twirl and drift, a frosty sea,
Whispering secrets of what might be.

Embers glow in a hearth's warm embrace,
Chasing away the cold's harsh trace.
Dreams flicker in the glowing light,
A haven found on this winter's night.

With every breath, the chill draws near,
Yet warmth surrounds, banishing fear.
In this moment, time stands still,
While outside, snowflakes gently spill.

Together they weave a tale so bright,
Of ember dreams that fill the night.
In shadows cast by the flick'ring flame,
A winter's whisper, never the same.

So let the snowflakes softly fall,
As dreams ignite by their crystal call.
In this embrace of cold and warm,
Life's fleeting moments take on a form.

A Gentle Flicker Amidst the Whispers of Frost

In the stillness of the night,
A gentle flicker brings delight.
Amongst the frosty breath of trees,
Soft murmurs carried on the breeze.

Candles sway in the evening glow,
Casting warmth where cold winds blow.
Each flame a beacon, tender light,
Guiding hearts through the endless night.

Whispers curl like mist in air,
Secrets held with loving care.
Stars peek through the crystal skies,
A tapestry where wonder lies.

Underneath the heavy boughs,
Nature sleeps, and time allows.
As dreams emerge from silent hope,
With gentle flickers, we learn to cope.

In the dance of frost and flame,
We find solace, not the same.
Moments weave a timeless thread,
In flick'rs of hope, our hearts are led.

Light from Within on a Winter's Eve

On a winter's eve so still,
The world awaits with snowy chill.
Yet in our hearts, a warmth does surge,
A light from within begins to merge.

Frosty windows, a gentle glow,
Whispers of love in soft tones flow.
Each flick'ring candle, a story shared,
Of dreams once scattered, now layered.

The night wraps close, a tender shawl,
As stars emerge, we heed their call.
For in the dark, hope takes its flight,
Finding solace in the quiet night.

Snowflakes pause on every ledge,
But warmth inside becomes the pledge.
To cherish moments, no matter how brief,
With light from within, we paint our belief.

So let the winter's chill enfold,
In hearts that gather, stories told.
With light that flickers, bright and true,
Love's warmth will guide, and see us through.

Soft Glistening Shadows at Twilight

At twilight's call, the day bids adieu,
Soft glistening shadows begin their cue.
Whispers of night weave in the air,
A tranquil scene beyond compare.

Golden hues fade to silver tones,
As daylight wanes, we hear the moans.
Voices of dusk in a tender sigh,
As stars emerge, dotting the sky.

The earth exhales its final breath,
Embracing stillness, yet eludes death.
Each shadow dances, a fleeting play,
In the soft glow of the fading day.

Silent moments twirl and glide,
While moonlight casts its silver tide.
With every heartbeat, time transcends,
In glistening shadows, the soul mends.

So let the twilight weave its spell,
In soft glistening shadows, we dwell.
As night unfolds its velvet sheet,
We find our place, forever sweet.

Ethereal Flames in the Stillness of Frost

In the hush where silence clings,
Ethereal flames dance and sing.
Whispers of warmth embrace the night,
Frost-kissed shadows take their flight.

Stars above begin to gleam,
Casting light like a fleeting dream.
In the stillness, hearts ignite,
Burning softly, pure and bright.

Each flicker tells a story told,
Of warmth within the bitter cold.
Flames entwine with the crystal air,
In beauty, we find solace there.

Embers glow with a gentle hue,
Painting the night in colors new.
The frost retreats from the fire's embrace,
As magic lingers in this place.

Let the ethereal warmth persist,
In the frost, we shall coexist.
As long as flames continue to rise,
Hope shall twinkle in starlit skies.

As the Night Grows Cold, Hearts Glow Warm

As the night claims the fading light,
Hearts awaken, ready for flight.
In the stillness, embraces grow,
Warming whispers, soft and low.

Beneath the moon's silver gaze,
Love ignites in a gentle blaze.
Frost may linger, sharp and keen,
But warmth within reigns supreme.

Candles flicker against the chill,
Each flame tells of love's great will.
In shadows, we find a place,
Where hearts unite in sweet embrace.

As the night weaves its icy thread,
We find comfort in warmth instead.
Beneath the frost, spirits rise,
Transforming chill into lullabies.

Together, we conquer the cold,
In every heartbeat, dreams unfold.
As night grows cold, let us stand,
With hearts aglow, hand in hand.

Flickering Hopes Under Icy Stars

Flickering hopes beneath the stars,
Amidst the night, we share our scars.
Each twinkle speaks of journeys long,
In icy air, our spirits throng.

Gentle breezes carry dreams,
While the moon bathes us in beams.
In this silence, fears dissolve,
As flickering flames begin to evolve.

Hope is born from freeze and thaw,
Quietly breaking winter's law.
Every spark ignites the dark,
Leading us through without a mark.

Stars watch over, steadfast and bright,
Guiding us towards the light.
With every breath, we rise and fall,
But flickering hopes shall conquer all.

So let us soar, united and free,
In the shadows, where hope can be.
Under icy stars, we find our way,
Embracing warmth in cold's ballet.

Solitary Warmth in a Frost-laden World

In a world where frost takes hold,
A solitary warmth unfolds.
One heart beats against the chill,
Defying winter's ruthless will.

Amidst the silence, embers glow,
Offering light in the bitter snow.
A single flame can spark a dream,
In the night's cold, softness streams.

Echoes linger where shadows fade,
Warmth emerges, not easily swayed.
Though frost may claim its rightful throne,
We find solace in the unknown.

Each breath a whisper, gently shared,
In the frost-laden world, we dared.
While winter's grip brings forth dismay,
Solitary warmth leads the way.

Our hearts, though solitary, shine,
Creating paths in lines divine.
For even in winter's cruelest fight,
A solitary warmth brings forth the light.

Chasing Warmth Through Crystal Air

In the breath of morning light,
I chase warmth through crystal air.
Frosty whispers in the bright,
A dance of joy, a hidden care.

Golden rays touch the earth's face,
While shadows linger, soft but near.
Nature's pulse, a gentle grace,
In this moment, time feels clear.

Footprints leading down the lane,
Each step a story to unfold.
Chasing warmth amidst the pain,
Hearts grow bold as dreams take hold.

The world sparkles, fresh and new,
With every breath, I find my song.
In the cold, my spirit flew,
Through the warmth, where I belong.

Together under skies so wide,
We seek the flame that unites.
Chasing warmth, with hearts as guides,
Through crystal air, we find our lights.

Glistening Shadows of Night's Embrace

In the silence, shadows play,
Glistening under pale moonlight.
Whispers weave in dark's ballet,
Embracing dreams that take their flight.

Stars like diamonds blink above,
Casting magic on the night.
With every breath, I feel the love,
In the shadows, pure delight.

Haunting echoes softly call,
As the wind begins to sigh.
In this stillness, I stand tall,
Bathed in stars that never die.

Veils of mist wrap around me,
In the dark, I find my way.
Glistening shadows set me free,
Guiding dreams that softly sway.

Night's embrace, a tender pull,
Leading hearts through tales untold.
In this hush, we're never dull,
Glistening shadows turn to gold.

Flickering Hues in the Winter Dark

Flickering hues dance with the night,
Painting whispers across the sky.
In winter's dark, there's soft delight,
A palette where warm spirits fly.

Crimson, gold, and shades of blue,
Merge in a tapestry of dreams.
Under stars that shine anew,
Hope lingers in gentle streams.

The crackle of leaves underfoot,
Echoes through a world so vast.
In the dark, we find our root,
Our flickering moment shall last.

Snowflakes twirl, a ballet slow,
In the air, they swirl and play.
Flickering hues, a silent glow,
Guiding our thoughts till break of day.

As the night begins to fade,
The dawn awaits with arms spread wide.
In winter's dark, we are remade,
Flickering hues, our cherished guide.

The Fire's Embrace in the Bitter Cold

In the hearth, the embers glow,
The fire's embrace warms the night.
Outside, the chill begins to grow,
Inside, we gather, hearts alight.

With every crackle, stories rise,
Of dreams woven with golden thread.
Flickering light in winter skies,
The warmth of love, our hearts are fed.

Through bitter winds that howl and bite,
We find solace in the flame.
Together here, we share our light,
In the dark, we call each name.

Laughter dances in the air,
The fire's glow a radiant guide.
Against the cold, we find our care,
In this moment, no need to hide.

The night grows deep, yet we feel bold,
Wrapped in warmth, we share our dreams.
The fire's embrace in bitter cold,
Ignites our souls with endless beams.

Glittering Echoes of a Fiery Breath

In twilight's embrace, embers dance bright,
Whispers of warmth in the folds of the night.
Flickering stars pulse, a fiery delight,
Carrying dreams on wings of the light.

Voices of passion pulse through the air,
Igniting the hearts, casting out despair.
With every breath, a story to share,
Glittering echoes that linger somewhere.

Vivid hues swirl in a passionate storm,
As vivid emotions begin to transform.
Burning desires in every warm form,
Fanning the flames as lost hopes reform.

In shadows that merge, a promise alive,
A flicker ignites, and the spirits thrive.
Through cracks in the dark, the embers contrive,
A symphony sung, making love to survive.

So dance with the fire, let it all unfold,
The echoes of warmth, a sight to behold.
For in every spark, a tale will be told,
Of glittering journeys, as shadows turn gold.

Healing Light Amongst the Frosted Trees

Beneath the boughs where silence weeps,
A gentle glow in the quiet creeps.
Healing whispers through branches steep,
In the frost, a promise, the lost it keeps.

Morning breaks with a tender kiss,
Soft rays peek through, bringing the bliss.
Among the snow, a moment of twist,
Life's revival in the air, it persists.

Brittle limbs cradle the light's embrace,
Nature's canvas painted with grace.
Each flicker a journey, a calming face,
Illuminating paths in a cold, vast space.

Through frozen breaths and crystal gaze,
The healing light carries through the maze.
As frost melts softly, the heart then plays,
Finding warmth in the chill's soft haze.

So linger here, where shadows recede,
Let the radiance flourish, fulfilling need.
In the silence, a promise, a blooming seed,
Amongst the trees, we find our creed.

Enchantment of Flames on Frosted Paths

On paths where whispers trace icy trails,
Flames awaken, telling ancient tales.
Dancing embers cast enchantment sails,
Illuminating dreams where silence prevails.

Frosted twilights, a canvas so bright,
Each flicker and glow, a beacon of light.
In the marriage of warmth, the cold takes flight,
Flames weave a spell, erasing the night.

Footsteps adorned with warmth and delight,
In the heart of the chill, love dances in sight.
Echoes of laughter make shadows ignite,
As flames flirt and twirl, a beautiful fight.

Snowflakes surrender to whispers of fire,
In the union of worlds, hearts leap ever higher.
Paths weave together, threads that inspire,
An enchantment of warmth that no one can tire.

So wander these roads, let the embers unfold,
In the heart of the frost, let the stories be told.
In the dance of the flames, the bold and the old,
Enchantment persists, where dreams are retold.

The Warm Glow of Life in an Icy World

Amidst the frost where shadows reside,
A warm glow arises, a beacon of pride.
In the chill of existence, hearts open wide,
Life pulses gently, a river, a tide.

Fingers of dawn stretch the night away,
With whispers of promise in each golden ray.
In the stillness of time, let the spirits sway,
Finding warmth in the cold, come what may.

Frost-kissed blossoms unfurl with the sun,
Each petal a story, a battle well won.
With radiant smiles, the shadows outrun,
In an icy world, life holds its fun.

Crystals of nature reflect in our eyes,
As warmth intertwines with the cold winter skies.
Every heartbeat echoes, a sweet surprise,
In the warmth of life, love never dies.

So cherish the glow, the pulse of the earth,
In the heart of the cold, find warmth and rebirth.
For in every flicker, a testament worth,
The warm glow of life, our eternal mirth.

Soft Glow Beneath Glistening Stars

In the stillness of the night,
A soft glow breaks the dark,
Whispers of dreams take flight,
As the universe leaves its mark.

Underneath the glittering sky,
Twinkling lights dance so bright,
Every sigh a gentle why,
In the quiet, souls unite.

Moments linger like a sigh,
Time slows with every breath,
In this space, we wonder why,
Finding peace beyond life and death.

The world fades in the dim light,
Wrapped in warmth, we find grace,
As stars blink in silent flight,
In this vast and endless space.

Hearts entwined, we softly glow,
Beneath the watchful eyes above,
In this stillness, love will grow,
In the quiet, we feel love.

The Warmth That Lingers in the Cold

Amidst the frost that bites the skin,
A warmth we seek, we find,
In the heart, where love begins,
A gentle touch, a binding kind.

The chill whispers secrets near,
Of twisting paths, of times once shared,
Yet in the shadows, hope draws near,
With kindred spirits, unprepared.

Fires flicker, casting dreams,
Embers glow through winter's shroud,
Together, we weave our schemes,
In this haven, joy is loud.

The snowflakes fall, a velvet guise,
Where laughter brings the sun's warm light,
Finding solace in each other's eyes,
As day turns softly into night.

Even in the season's bite,
Our hearts shall hold the summer's sway,
The warmth within lasts through the night,
As love will always find a way.

Secrets of the Flame in the Frigid Air

In the stillness, secrets whisper,
Of flames that dance in icy breath,
Each flicker tells a tale crisper,
Of life and warmth beyond the death.

A bond ignited in the freeze,
Hidden truths within the light,
Crackling sounds, a gentle tease,
As shadows whisper of the night.

The cold may cling, but hearts ignite,
With every spark, we push through fear,
Embracing warmth, we feel just right,
In this moment, love draws near.

We gather close, our stories shared,
The flames reflect our hopes and fears,
In every glance, we are prepared,
To face the world throughout the years.

In the dark, ignite the flame,
With every heartbeat, life anew,
As long as we can share the same,
The secrets sung in warmth's soft hue.

Glow of Solace in a Frozen World

Amidst the chill of winter's grace,
A glow emerges in the dark,
Breath of solace, a warm embrace,
A tender light, a hopeful spark.

The world is dressed in white and gray,
Yet in our hearts, the colors bloom,
In each laugh, we find our way,
As joy ignites the frozen gloom.

Moments shimmer like fresh snow,
With every step, our spirits rise,
In harmony, we start to flow,
As warmth ignites in winter's guise.

Gentle whispers fill the air,
In every glance, solace is found,
Together, we shed every care,
As love's embrace wraps all around.

So let the frost reign all around,
For in our hearts, the glow remains,
In this frozen world, we'll be found,
Where love endures through winter's chains.

Echoes of Warmth Beneath the Snow

In silence white, the world unfolds,
Soft whispers dance, as winter holds.
Beneath the chill, a spark remains,
Echoes of warmth in frosted lanes.

Footprints trace a tale of light,
Through snowy paths, a heart ignites.
Each gentle flake, a fleeting kiss,
Reminds us all of love's pure bliss.

The trees stand tall, adorned in white,
Roots embrace the earth so tight.
Yet in the cold, life stirs below,
Where echoes of warmth begin to grow.

The hearth within, a longing glow,
Calls us close, where spirits flow.
In every heart, a flicker bright,
Guides us through the longest night.

Shimmering Nights with a Warm Glare

Underneath the velvet sky,
Stars like lanterns flicker high.
A gentle breeze stirs dreams anew,
In shimmering nights, the warmth shines through.

With every breath, the cosmos hums,
Where quiet moments softly come.
Golden rays through windows play,
In tender glow, the world holds sway.

The moonlight bathes the earth in lace,
A tranquil night, a sweet embrace.
Each shadow whispers tales of yore,
With warmth that lingers, forevermore.

In gatherings near, the laughter flows,
Amongst the stars, the spirit grows.
Together we bask, in joys we share,
In shimmering nights, with a warm glare.

Hearth Fire in the Depth of Winter

In winter's grasp, the world stands still,
A hearth fire crackles, a warm thrill.
The flames dance high, as shadows play,
Chasing the chill of the fading day.

Cups brim with warmth, stories unfold,
Embers glow bright, against the cold.
From distant lands, our hearts align,
In the warmth of fire, our souls entwine.

The snow drapes gently, a soft white quilt,
Yet here, together, love is built.
With every laugh, our spirits soar,
Hearth fire magic, we crave more.

Outside's a world of icy breath,
Yet here, we find our sacred rest.
In the depth of winter, bonds so tight,
The hearth fire blazes, bright in the night.

The Gleam Beneath the Frost

In the quiet dawn, a treasure glows,
The gleam beneath, where beauty flows.
Frosted leaves, a silvery dance,
Whispering tales of nature's chance.

Beneath the cold, life stirs awake,
In fragile forms, the earth will shake.
Through icy panes, a light breaks free,
Unveiling warmth, as hearts can see.

The chill may bite, yet love persists,
In every moment, the heart insists.
The gleam beneath reveals our way,
Guiding us through the wintry gray.

Nature's art, a wondrous sight,
Beneath the frost, a spark ignites.
So as we tread on paths of white,
We find the gleam, our shared delight.

Luminous Reflections in a Snowy Realm

In a world of white so bright,
Stars watch over in the night.
Snowflakes twirl in a gentle breeze,
Whispers dance among the trees.

Moonlight glimmers on the ground,
A soft hush, a sacred sound.
Crystals sparkle in their flight,
Nature's artistry ignites the night.

The chilly air, a sweet embrace,
Each breath visible in this space.
Footprints traced where few have been,
Silence spoken, deep within.

Trees wear coats of icy lace,
Winter's breath, a fleeting grace.
Reflections shimmer, pale and clear,
Luminous dreams drift ever near.

Imprints of joy across the snow,
A tapestry where hopes will grow.
In this realm of frost and light,
Hearts unite in pure delight.

Shimmering Nightfall and Frosted Air

As daylight fades to twilight hue,
Shadows stretch, the darkness grew.
Stars awaken, one by one,
Whispers of the night begun.

Frosted air, a breath so cold,
Tales of winter, quietly told.
Moonbeams dance on silver streams,
Catching echoes of our dreams.

Branches crackle under weight,
Nature's beauty, in a state.
Each exhale, a cloud of grace,
In this still and sacred place.

Twinkling lights in every street,
Where life's rhythm finds its beat.
Winter's magic, soft and rare,
Every moment filled with care.

Shimmering night, a canvas wide,
Stars as secrets, none can hide.
Frosted dreams, in the night air,
Hope and love, a gentle prayer.

A Glow Against the Icy Veil

In the heart of winter's freeze,
A glow emerges with such ease.
Light and dark in soft embrace,
A dance within this frozen space.

Candles flicker in the basins,
Shadows whisper of creations.
Fires crackle, warmth ignites,
Bringing solace on long nights.

Through frosted panes, the light it flows,
Casting brilliance on the snow.
Each reflection sparks a dream,
In this world of silver gleam.

Beneath the branches, soft and deep,
Nature's lullaby, we keep.
In the glow, our spirits mend,
Against the night, our hearts can blend.

So let the winter winds a-whirl,
With every heartbeat, our hopes unfurl.
A glow against the icy veil,
In this wonder, we shall sail.

Winter's Dance of Flame and Ice

In the chill of winter's breath,
Life and warmth defy the death.
Fires crackle, hearts ignite,
In the dance of day and night.

Flames leap high, a fiery glow,
While outside, the cold winds blow.
Ice like diamonds, rare and bold,
Nature's beauty to behold.

Footsteps crunch on snowy trails,
As winter tells its quiet tales.
A harmony of warmth and chill,
In this world, time seems to still.

Twirling flames and frosty air,
In this dance, we find our care.
Moments shared by light and dark,
Through the stillness, love can spark.

Every season brings a song,
With every note, we all belong.
Winter's dance, a fierce embrace,
Flame and ice, a timeless grace.

Milton Keynes UK
Ingram Content Group UK Ltd.
UKHW010230111224
452348UK00011B/637